EASY GUITAR

THE BEST SONGS EVER

6TH EDITION

ISBN 978-1-5400-2237-0

HAL•LEONARD®

Visit Hal Leonard Online at
www.halleonard.com

Contact Us:
Hal Leonard
7777 West Bluemound Road
Milwaukee, WI 53213
Email: info@halleonard.com

In Europe contact:
Hal Leonard Europe Limited
42 Wigmore Street
Marylebone, London, W1U 2RN
Email: info@halleonardeurope.com

In Australia contact:
Hal Leonard Australia Pty. Ltd.
4 Lentara Court
Cheltenham, Victoria, 3192 Australia
Email: info@halleonard.com.au

STRUM AND PICK PATTERNS

This chart contains the suggested strum and pick patterns that are referred to by number at the beginning of each song in this book. The symbols ⊓ and ∨ in the strum patterns refer to down and up strokes, respectively. The letters in the pick patterns indicate which right-hand fingers play which strings.

p = thumb
i = index finger
m = middle finger
a = ring finger

For example; Pick Pattern 2
is played: thumb - index - middle - ring

You can use the 3/4 Strum and Pick Patterns in songs written in compound meter (6/8, 9/8, 12/8, etc.). For example, you can accompany a song in 6/8 by playing the 3/4 pattern twice in each measure. The 4/4 Strum and Pick Patterns can be used for songs written in cut time (¢) by doubling the note time values in the patterns. Each pattern would therefore last two measures in cut time.

All I Ask of You

from THE PHANTOM OF THE OPERA

Music by Andrew Lloyd Webber
Lyrics by Charles Hart
Additional Lyrics by Richard Stilgoe

Strum Pattern: 1, 2
Pick Pattern: 2, 4

Verse
Slow

1. No more talk of dark-ness, for - get these wide - eyed fears; I'm
2. *See additional lyrics*

here, noth-ing can harm you, my words will warm and calm you. Let me be your free-dom, let

day - light dry your tears; I'm here with you, be - side you, to guard you and to guide you.

Chorus

1. All I ask is ev - 'ry wak - ing mo - ment, turn my head with talk of
2., 3. *See additional lyrics*

sum - mer - time. Say you need me with you now and al - ways;

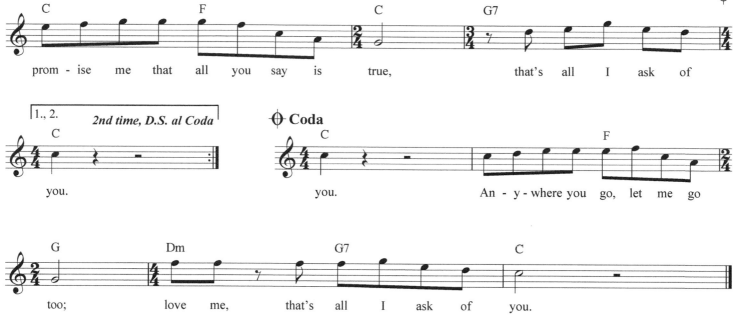

prom - ise me that all you say is true, that's all I ask of

1., 2.
2nd time, D.S. al Coda

⊕ Coda

you.

you.

An - y - where you go, let me go

too;   love me, that's all I ask of you.

Additional Lyrics

2. Let me be your shelter, let me be your light;
You're safe, no one will find you, your fears are far behind you.
All I want is freedom, a world with no more night;
And you, always beside me, to hold me and to hide me.

Chorus 2. Then say you'll share with me one love, one lifetime.
Let me lead you from your solitude.
Say you need me with you, here, beside you.
Anywhere you go, let me go too.
Christine, that's all I ask of you.

Chorus 3. All I ask for is one love, one lifetime.
Say the word and I will follow you.
Share each day with me each night, each morning.
Say you love me! You know I do.
Love me, that's all I ask of you.

At Last

from ORCHESTRA WIVES

Lyric by Mack Gordon
Music by Harry Warren

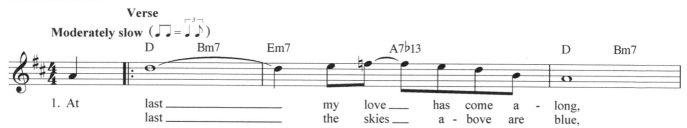

Strum Pattern: 3
Pick Pattern: 3

Verse
Moderately slow

1. At   last _____   my   love ____   has   come   a - long,
   last _____   the   skies ____   a - bove   are   blue,

All the Things You Are

from VERY WARM FOR MAY

Lyrics by Oscar Hammerstein II
Music by Jerome Kern

Strum Pattern: 3
Pick Pattern: 5

Always

Words and Music by Irving Berlin

Bewitched

from PAL JOEY
Words by Lorenz Hart
Music by Richard Rodgers

Billie Jean

Words and Music by Michael Jackson

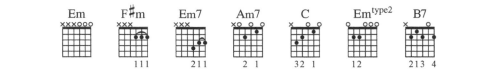

Strum Pattern: 1, 2
Pick Pattern: 2, 4

1. She was more like a beau - ty queen from a mov - ie scene. I said don't mind, but what do
2. *See additional lyrics*

____ you mean I ____ am the one ____ who will dance ____ on the floor ____ in the round? ____

She said I ____ am the one ____ who will dance ____

on the floor _ in the round. _ She told me her name was Bil-

- lie Jean as she caused a scene. Then ev - 'ry head turned with eyes __ that dreamed of be - ing the one _

_ who will dance __ on the floor _ in the round. _

Pre-Chorus

Peo-ple al - ways told me, be care-ful of what you do. _ Uh, don't go a - round _ break-in' young girls' hearts. _
See additional lyrics

_ And Moth - er al - ways told me, be care-ful of who you love. _ And be

Chorus

care-ful of what you do, __ 'cause the lie be - comes _ the truth. Hey! _____ Bil - lie Jean _ is

not my lov - er. She's just a girl ___ who claims that I ___ am the one, ___

___ but the kid ___ is not my son. ___ She says I ___ am the one, ___

___ but the kid ___ is not my son. ___

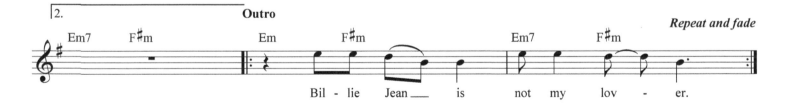

Outro *Repeat and fade*

Bil - lie Jean ___ is not my lov - er.

Additional Lyrics

2. For forty days and for forty nights,
Law was on her side.
But who can stand when she's in demand,
Her schemes and plans,
'Cause we danced on the floor in the round?
So take my strong advice:
Just remember to always think twice.
She told me my baby, we danced till three,
And then she looked at me, then showed a photo.
My baby cried. His eyes were like mine,
'Cause we dance on the floor in the round.

Pre-Chorus People always told me, be careful of what you do.
Uh, don't go around breakin' young girls' hearts.
But you came and stood right by me,
Just a smell of sweet perfume.
This happened much too soon.
She called me to her room. Hey!

Body and Soul

Words by Edward Heyman, Robert Sour and Frank Eyton
Music by John Green

Strum Pattern: 4
Pick Pattern: 5

Additional Lyrics

2. I spend my days in longing
   And wond'ring why it's me you're wronging,
   I tell you I mean it,
   I'm all for you, body and soul!

3. My life a wreck you're making,
   You know I'm yours for just the taking;
   I'll gladly surrender
   Myself to you, body and soul!

Blue Skies

from BETSY

Words and Music by Irving Berlin

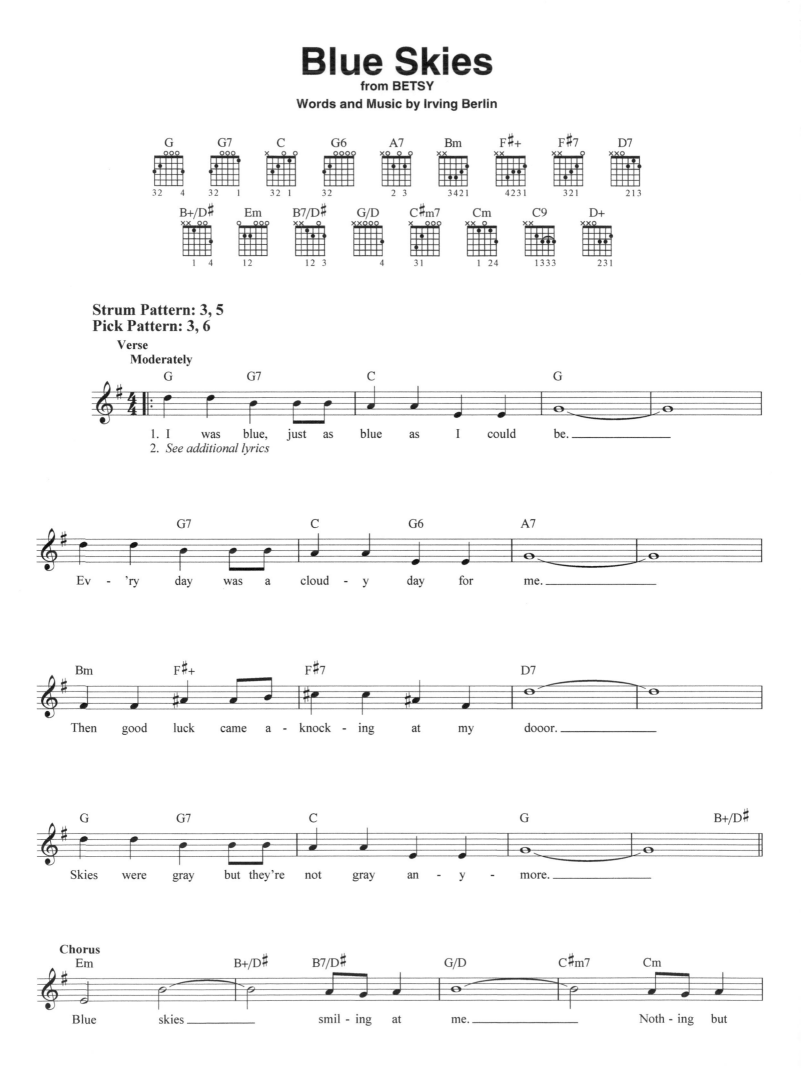

Strum Pattern: 3, 5
Pick Pattern: 3, 6

Verse
Moderately

1. I was blue, just as blue as I could be. _____
2. *See additional lyrics*

Ev - 'ry day was a cloud - y day for me. _____

Then good luck came a - knock - ing at my dooor. _____

Skies were gray but they're not gray an - y - more. _____

Chorus

Blue skies _____ smil - ing at me. _____ Noth - ing but

Additional Lyrics

2. I should care if the wind blows east or west.
   I should fret if the worst looks like the best.
   I should mind if they say it can't be true.
   I should smile if that's exactly what I do.

Can't Help Falling in Love

from the Paramount Picture BLUE HAWAII

Words and Music by George David Weiss, Hugo Peretti and Luigi Creatore

Strum Pattern: 2
Pick Pattern: 4

Additional Lyrics

2. Shall I stay?
   Would it be a sin
   If I can't help falling in love with you?

Candle in the Wind

Words and Music by Elton John and Bernie Taupin

Strum Pattern: 3
Pick Pattern: 2

Verse
Moderately, in 2

1. Good-bye, Nor - ma Jean. _____ Though I nev - er knew you _ at all, _____
2., 3. *See additional lyrics*

_____ you had the grace to hold _____ your - self _____ while those a - round _ you crawled. _____

They crawled out of the wood-work and they whis - pered

in - to _____ your brain. _____ They set you _____ on a tread - mill and they

‹♦› **Coda**

Your can - dle burned _ out long be - fore _ your

leg - end ev - er did. _____

Additional Lyrics

2. Loneliness was tough, the toughest role you ever played.
   Hollywood created a superstar and pain was the price you paid.
   And even when you died, oh, the press still hounded you.
   All the papers had to say was that Marilyn was found in the nude.

3. Goodbye, Norma Jean. Though I never knew you at all,
   You had the grace to hold yourself while those around you crawled.
   Goodbye, Norma Jean, from a young man in the twenty-second row,
   Who sees you as something more than sexual, more than just our Marilyn Monroe.

Defying Gravity

from the Broadway Musical WICKED
Music and Lyrics by Stephen Schwartz

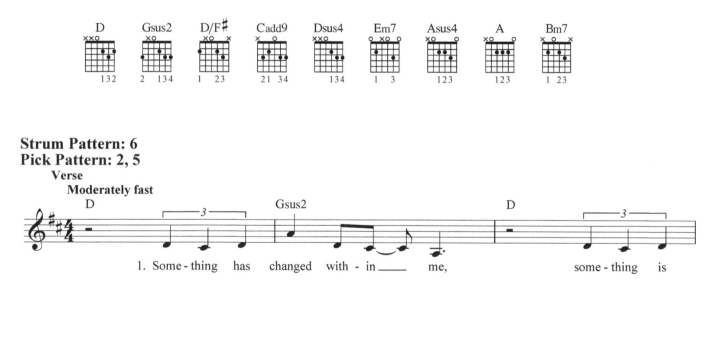

Strum Pattern: 6
Pick Pattern: 2, 5

Verse
Moderately fast

1. Some - thing has changed with - in ___ me, some - thing is

not the same. I'm through with play - ing by ___ the rules ___ of some - one

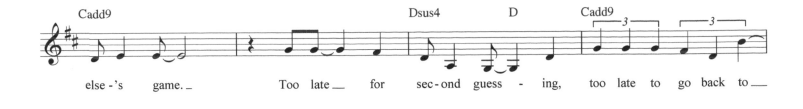

else-'s game. ___ Too late ___ for sec-ond guess - ing, too late to go back to ___

___ sleep. ___ It's time ___ to trust my in - stincts, close my eyes ___ and

leap… ___ It's time ___ to try de - fy - ing grav - i - ty. ___

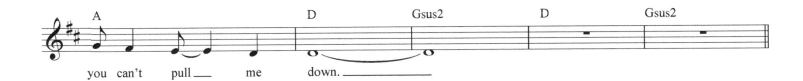

___ I think ___ I'll try de - fy - ing grav - i - ty, and

you can't pull ___ me down. ___

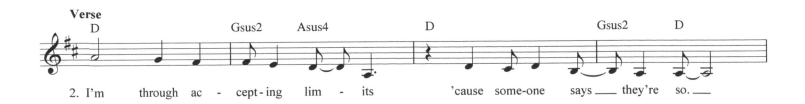

2. I'm through ac - cept-ing lim - its 'cause some-one says ___ they're so. ___

Crazy

Words and Music by Willie Nelson

Edelweiss

from THE SOUND OF MUSIC

Lyrics by Oscar Hammerstein II
Music by Richard Rodgers

Strum Pattern: 7
Pick Pattern: 7

Every Breath You Take

Music and Lyrics by Sting

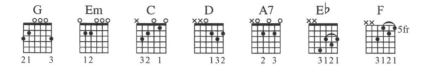

Strum Pattern: 4
Pick Pattern: 3

How my poor heart __ aches _____ with ev-'ry step __ you take.

Verse

3., 4. Ev-'ry move you __ make, ev-'ry vow you __ break,

ev-'ry smile __ you fake, ev-'ry claim __ you stake, I'll be watch-ing you. __

To Coda ⊕

Bridge

Since you've gone __ I been lost __

__ with-out __ a trace, I dream at night I can on - ly see __ your face.

I look a-round but it's you I can't __ re-place, I feel so cold and I

long for your __ em-brace. I keep cry-ing ba - by, ba - by, please. __

Interlude

D.S. al Coda

✛ **Coda**

Oh, can't you __

Ev - 'ry move __ you make, ev - 'ry step __ you take,

Outro

I'll be watch - ing you. _____

I'll be watch - ing you. _____

Additional Lyrics

2. Ev'ry single day, ev'ry word you say,
   Ev'ry game you play, ev'ry night you stay,
   I'll be watching you.

I Dreamed a Dream

from LES MISERABLES

Music by Claude-Michel Schönberg
Lyrics by Alain Boublil, Jean-Marc Natel and Herbert Kretzmer

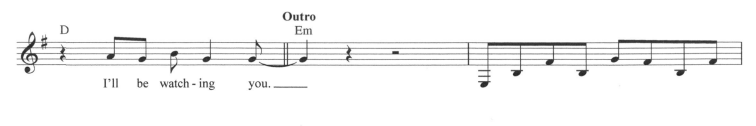

Strum Pattern: 1
Pick Pattern: 2

Verse
Moderately

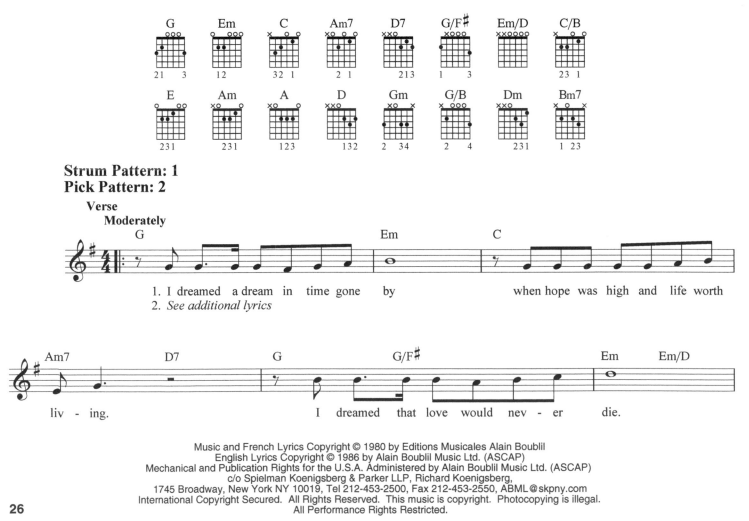

1. I dreamed a dream in time gone by   when hope was high and life worth
2. *See additional lyrics*

liv - ing.   I dreamed that love would nev - er die.

Outro-Verse

And still I dreamed he'd come to me, that we would live the years to-geth-er. But there are dreams that can-not be, and there are storms we can-not weath-er. I had a dream my life would be so dif-f'rent from this hell I'm liv-ing, so dif-f'rent now from what it seemed. Now life has killed the dream I dreamed.

Additional Lyrics

2. Then I was young and unafraid,
   So, dreams were made and used and wasted.
   There was no ransom to be paid,
   No song unsung, no wine untasted.

Fly Me to the Moon
(In Other Words)

Words and Music by Bart Howard

Strum Pattern: 3, 4
Pick Pattern: 3, 4

TRO - © Copyright 1954 (Renewed) Palm Valley Music, L.L.C., New York, NY
International Copyright Secured
All Rights Reserved Including Public Performance For Profit
Used by Permission

Georgia on My Mind

Words by Stuart Gorrell
Music by Hoagy Carmichael

The Girl from Ipanema
(Garôta de Ipanema)

Music by Antonio Carlos Jobim
English Words by Norman Gimbel
Original Words by Vinicius De Moraes

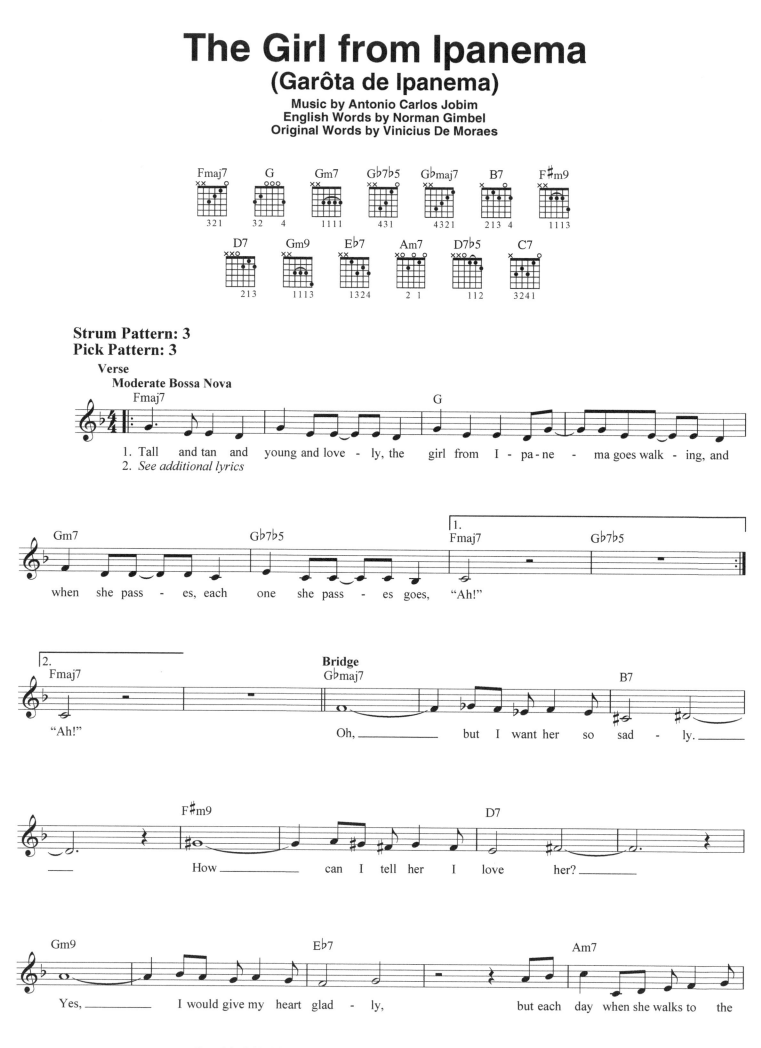

Additional Lyrics

2. When she walks she's like a samba
That swings so cool and sways so gentle,
That when she passes,
Each one she passes goes, "Ah!"

Imagine

Words and Music by John Lennon

Strum Pattern: 1
Pick Pattern: 2

Additional Lyrics

3. Imagine no possessions,
   I wonder if you can;
   No need for greed or hunger,
   A brotherhood of man.
   Imagine all the people sharing all the world.

Hallelujah

Words and Music by Leonard Cohen

C   Am   F   G   E7

Strum Pattern: 9
Pick Pattern: 9

Verse
Moderately slow, in 2

1. Well, I heard there was a se-cret chord ___ that Da-vid played ___ and it
2.–5. *See additional lyrics*

pleased the Lord, but you don't ___ real-ly care for mu-sic, do ya? ___

Well, it goes like this: the fourth, the fifth, the mi-nor fall, ___ and the

ma-jor lift, the baf-fled king ___ com-pos - ing ___ Hal-le-

Chorus

lu-jah. ___ Hal-le-lu-jah, ___ hal-le-

Additional Lyrics

2. Well, your faith was strong, but you needed proof.
   You saw her bathing on the roof.
   Her beauty and the moonlight overthrew ya.
   She tied you to her kitchen chair,
   And she broke your throne and she cut your hair,
   And from your lips she drew the hallelujah.

3. Well, baby, I've been here before,
   I've seen this room and I've walked this floor.
   You know, I used to live alone before I knew ya.
   And I've seen your flag on the marble arch,
   And love is not a vict'ry march,
   It's a cold and it's a broken hallelujah.

4. Well, there was a time when you let me know
   What's really going on below.
   But now you never show that to me, do ya?
   But remember when I moved in you
   And the holy dove was moving too,
   And ev'ry breath we drew was hallelujah.

5. Maybe there is a God above,
   But all I've ever learned from love
   Was how to shoot somebody who outdrew ya.
   And it's not a cry that you hear at night,
   It's not somebody who's seen the light,
   It's a cold and it's a broken hallelujah.

Happy

from DESPICABLE ME 2
Words and Music by Pharrell Williams

_____ you feel like a room with-out a roof. _____ (Be-cause I'm

hap-py.) Clap a-long if_____ you feel_____ like hap-pi-ness is the truth. _____

_____ (Be-cause I'm hap-py.) Clap a-long_____ if_____ you know what

hap-pi-ness is to you. _____ (Be-cause I'm hap-py.) Clap a-long if_____

_____ you feel_____ like that's what you wan - na do. _____

𝄉 Bridge

Bring me down, _____ can't noth-in' bring me down; _____

_____ your love is too high. Bring me down, _____ can't noth-in'

Here's That Rainy Day

from CARNIVAL IN FLANDERS

Words by Johnny Burke
Music by Jimmy Van Heusen

Hey Jude

Words and Music by John Lennon and Paul McCartney

Strum Pattern: 2
Pick Pattern: 4

Additional Lyrics

2. Hey Jude, don't be afraid,
   You were made to go out and get her.
   The minute you let her under your skin,
   Then you begin to make it better.

Bridge So let it out and let it in,
   Hey Jude, begin,
   You're waiting for someone to perform with.
   And don't you know that it's just you?
   Hey Jude, you'll do, the movement you need
   Is on your shoulder. Na, na, na, na, na, na, na, na, na.

How Deep Is the Ocean
(How High Is the Sky)

Words and Music by Irving Berlin

Strum Pattern: 4
Pick Pattern: 1

I Will Always Love You

Words and Music by Dolly Parton

Strum Pattern: 3, 4
Pick Pattern: 3, 4

Additional Lyrics

2. Bittersweet memories,
   That's all I am taking with me.
   Goodbye, please don't cry.
   We both know that I'm not what you need.
   But...

3. *Spoken:* I hope life treats you kind.
   And I hope that you have
   All that you ever dreamed of.
   And I wish you joy and happiness,
   But above all this, I wish you love.
   And...

I Left My Heart in San Francisco

Words by Douglass Cross
Music by George Cory

I'll Be Seeing You

from RIGHT THIS WAY

Written by Irving Kahal and Sammy Fain

Strum Pattern: 1, 3
Pick Pattern: 2, 3

The Lady Is a Tramp

from BABES IN ARMS

Words by Lorenz Hart
Music by Richard Rodgers

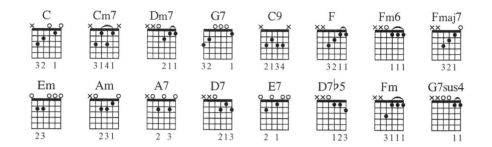

Strum Pattern: 2, 3
Pick Pattern: 3, 4

Verse
Moderately

C / Cm7 / Dm7 / G7

1., 3. I get too hun - gry for din - ner at eight. ____
2., 4. *See additional lyrics*

C / Cm7 / Dm7 / G7 / C

I like the thea - tre but nev - er come late. ____ I nev - er

C9 / F / Fm6 / C / Dm7 / G7

both - er with peo - ple I hate. ____ That's why the la - dy is a

1., 3.
C / G7

tramp. ____

2., 4.
C / N.C.

tramp. ____ I like the free fresh

Bridge
Fmaj7 / G7

Em / Am / Dm7 / G7 / C / A7 / D7 / G7

wind in my hair, ____ life with-out care. ____ I'm broke, it's oke.

Outro

To Coda ⊕

C / Cm7 / Dm7 / E7 / Am

Hate Cal - i - for - nia, it's cold and it's damp. ____ That's why the

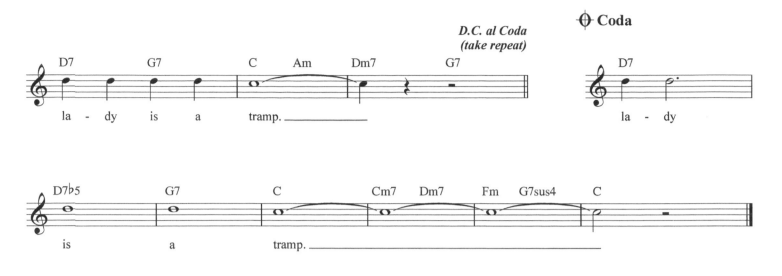

D.C. al Coda
(take repeat)

⊕ Coda

| D7 | G7 | C Am Dm7 | G7 |

la - dy is a tramp. _____

| D7 |

la - dy

| D7♭5 | G7 | C | Cm7 Dm7 | Fm G7sus4 | C |

is a tramp. _____

Additional Lyrics

2., 4. I don't like crap games with Barons and Earls,
Won't go to Harlem in ermine and pearls.
Won't dish the dirt with the rest of the girls,
That's why the lady is a tramp.

Night and Day

from GAY DIVORCE

Words and Music by Cole Porter

B♭maj7 A7 Dmaj7 G♯m7♭5 Gm7 F♯m7 F°7 Em7 Fmaj7 D

Strum Pattern: 3, 4
Pick Pattern: 1, 3

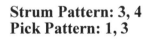

Verse

Moderately

| B♭maj7 | A7 | Dmaj7 |

1. Night and day _____ you are the one. _____ On - ly you ___

2. *See additional lyrics*

| B♭maj7 | A7 | Dmaj7 |

___ be - neath ___ the moon ___ and un - der the sun. _____ Wheth - er

Additional Lyrics

2. Day and night, why is it so
   That this longing for you follows wherever I go?
   In the roaring traffic's boom, in the silence of my lonely room,
   I think of you, night and day.

Isn't It Romantic?

from the Paramount Picture LOVE ME TONIGHT

Words by Lorenz Hart
Music by Richard Rodgers

Strum Pattern: 4, 5
Pick Pattern: 4, 5

Additional Lyrics

2. My face is glowing, I'm energetic, the art of sewing, I found poetic.
My needle punctuates the rhythm of romance! I don't give a stitch if I don't get rich.
A custom tailor who has no custom is like a sailor, no one will trust 'em.
But there is magic in the music of my shears; I shed no tears. Lend me your ears!

Chorus Isn't it romantic? Soon I will have found some girl that I adore.
Isn't it romantic? While I sit around, my love can scrub the floor.
She'll kiss me ev'ry hour, or she'll get the sack.
And when I take a shower she can scrub my back.
Isn't it romantic? On a moonlight night she'll cook me onion soup.
Kiddies are romantic, and if we don't fight, we soon will have a troop!
We'll help the population, it's a duty that we owe to dear old France.
Isn't it romance?

It Might As Well Be Spring

from STATE FAIR

Lyrics by Oscar Hammerstein II
Music by Richard Rodgers

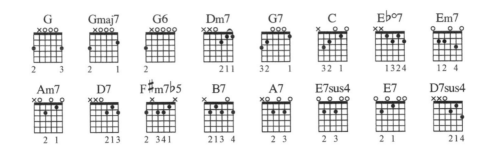

Strum Pattern: 2, 3
Pick Pattern: 3, 4

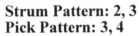

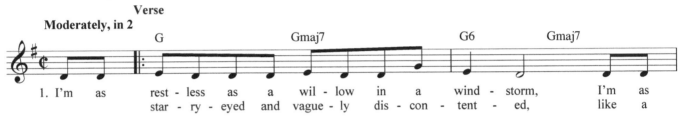

1. I'm as rest-less as a wil-low in a wind-storm, I'm as
star-ry-eyed and vague-ly dis-con-tent-ed, like a

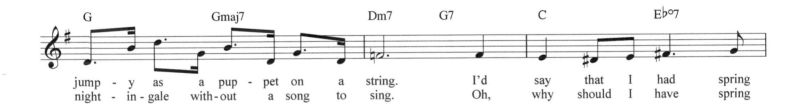

jump-y as a pup-pet on a string. I'd say that I had spring
night-in-gale with-out a song to sing. Oh, why should I have spring

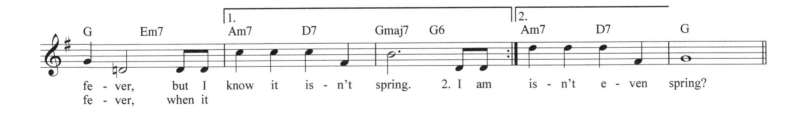

fe-ver, but I know it is-n't spring. 2. I am is-n't e-ven spring?
fe-ver, when it

I keep wish-ing I were some-where else, walk-ing down a strange, new

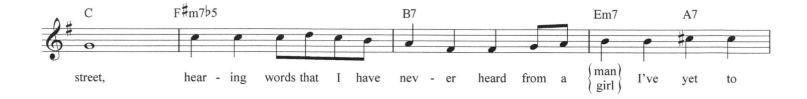

street, hear - ing words that I have nev - er heard from a {man / girl} I've yet to

Outro-Verse

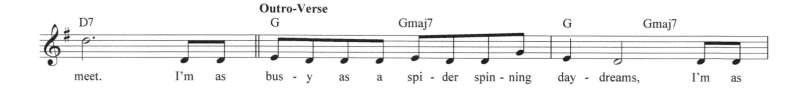

meet. I'm as bus - y as a spi - der spin - ning day - dreams, I'm as

gid - dy as a ba - by on a swing. I have - n't seen a cro - cus or a

rose - bud or a rob - in on the wing, but I feel so gay in a

mel - an - chol - y way that it might as well be spring. It

might _____ as well _____ be spring! _____

Just the Way You Are

Words and Music by Billy Joel

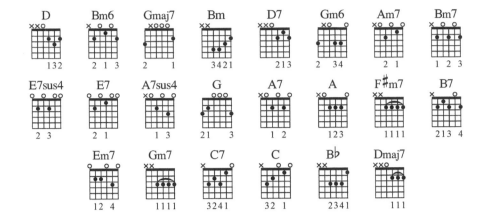

Strum Pattern: 1
Pick Pattern: 2

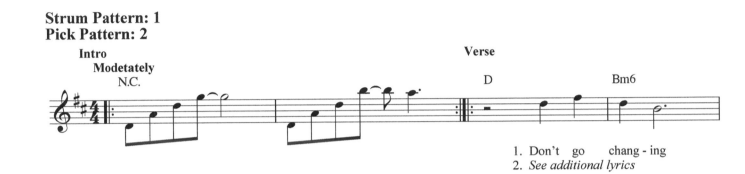

Intro
Modetately
N.C.

Verse
D   Bm6

1. Don't go chang - ing
2. *See additional lyrics*

Gmaj7   Bm   D7   Gmaj7   Gm6   D

to try and please me,   you nev - er let me down _ be - fore.

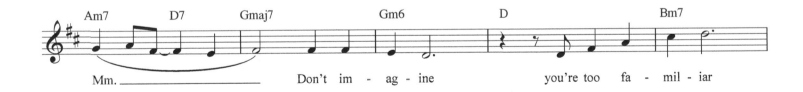

Am7   D7   Gmaj7   Gm6   D   Bm7

Mm. _____   Don't im - ag - ine   you're too fa - mil - iar

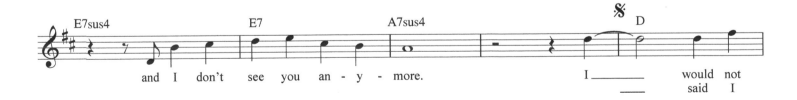

E7sus4   E7   A7sus4   %   D

and I don't see you an - y - more.   I _____ would not
                                            ____ said I

Bm6   Gmaj7   Bm   D7   Gmaj7   Gm6

leave you   in times of trou - ble,   we nev - er could have come _ this
love you   and that's for - ev - er,   and this I prom - ise from _ the

Additional Lyrics

2. Don't go trying some new fashion,
Don't change the color of your hair. Mm.
You always have my unspoken passion,
Although I might not seem to care.
I don't want clever conversation,
I never want to work that hard. Mm.
I just want someone that I can talk to;
I want you just the way you are.

Let It Be

Words and Music by John Lennon and Paul McCartney

Strum Pattern: 3
Pick Pattern: 4

% Verse

Slow

1. When I find my-self in times of trou-ble, Moth-er Mar - y comes to me,
3. *Instrumental*

speak-ing words of wis - dom, let it be. And in my hour of dark - ness, she is

stand-ing right in front of me, speak-ing words of wis - dom, let it be. *Instrumental ends* Let it be,

Chorus

let it be, let it be, let it be. Whis-per words of wis-dom, let it be.

Let It Be Me
(Je T'appartiens)

English Words by Mann Curtis
French Words by Pierre DeLanoe
Music by Gilbert Becaud

Strum Pattern: 3
Pick Pattern: 3, 5

Love Me Tender

Words and Music by Elvis Presley and Vera Matson

Strum Pattern: 4
Pick Pattern: 6

Verse
Slow

1. Love me ten - der, love me sweet, nev - er let me go. You have made my
2. *See additional lyrics*

life com - plete, and I love you so.

Chorus
Love me ten - der, love me true,

all my dreams ful - fill. For, my dar - lin', I love you, and I al - ways will.

Verse

3. Love me ten - der, love me dear, tell me you are mine. I'll be yours through

Outro-Chorus
all the years, till the end of time. Love me ten - der, love me true,

all my dreams ful - fill. For, my dar - lin', I love you, and I al - ways will.

Additional Lyrics

2. Love me tender, love me long,
   Take me to your heart.
   For it's there that I belong,
   And we'll never part.

Love Walked In

from GOLDWYN FOLLIES

Music and Lyrics by George Gershwin and Ira Gershwin

Strum Pattern: 3, 4
Pick Pattern: 3, 4

Moon River

from the Paramount Picture BREAKFAST AT TIFFANY'S
Words by Johnny Mercer
Music by Henry Mancini

Memory

from CATS

Music by Andrew Lloyd Webber
Text by Trevor Nunn after T.S. Eliot

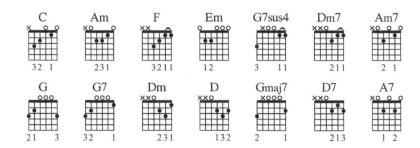

Additional Lyrics

2. Mem'ry all alone in the moonlight,
I can smile at the old days.
I was beautiful then.
I remember the time I knew what happiness was.
Let the mem'ry live again.

Bridge Burnt out ends of smoky days,
The stale cold smell of morning.
The street lamp dies, another night is over.
Another day is dawning.

4. Touch me. It's so easy to leave me
All alone with this mem'ry of my days in the sun.
If you touch me, you'll understand what happiness is.
Look, a new day has begun.

Moonlight in Vermont

Words by John Blackburn
Music by Karl Suessdorf

Strum Pattern: 4
Pick Pattern: 5

Additional Lyrics

2. Icy fingerwaves,
   Ski trails on a mountainside,
   Snowlight in Vermont.

3. Ev'ning summer breeze,
   Warbling of a meadowlark,
   Moonlight in Vermont.

My Favorite Things

from THE SOUND OF MUSIC

Lyrics by Oscar Hammerstein II
Music by Richard Rodgers

Additional Lyrics

2. Cream colored ponies and crisp apple strudels,
   Doorbells and sleighbells and schnitzel with noodles,
   Wild geese that fly with the moon on their wings,
   These are a few of my favorite things.

My Funny Valentine

from BABES IN ARMS
Words by Lorenz Hart
Music by Richard Rodgers

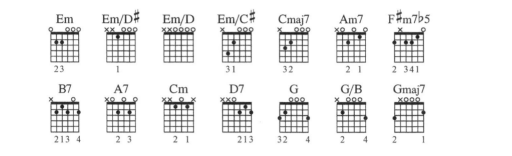

Strum Pattern: 4
Pick Pattern: 5

My Heart Will Go On
(Love Theme From 'Titanic')
from the Paramount and Twentieth Century Fox Motion Picture TITANIC

Music by James Horner
Lyric by Will Jennings

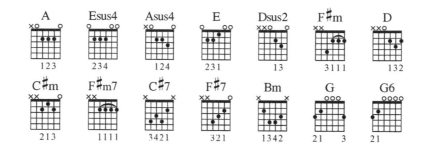

Strum Pattern: 3
Pick Pattern: 3

Verse
Moderately

1. Ev - 'ry night in my dreams I see you, I feel you, that is how I

know you go on. Far a-cross the dis - tance and spac - es be -

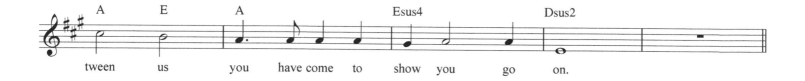

tween us you have come to show you go on.

%Chorus

Near, far, wher - ev - er you are, ___ I be - lieve that the

To Coda ⊕

Verse

D.S. al Coda

My Way

English Words by Paul Anka
Original French Words by Gilles Thibault
Music by Jacques Revaux and Claude Francois

Strum Pattern: 3, 4
Pick Pattern: 2, 5

Intro
Moderately slow

Verse

1. And now the end is
2. *See additional lyrics*

near and so I face the fi-nal cur-tain. ___ My friend, I'll say it

clear, I'll state my case of which I'm cer-tain. ___ I've lived a life that's

full. I've trav-eled each and ev-'ry high-way. And more, much more than

Additional Lyrics

2. Regrets, I've had a few, but then again, too few to mention.
I did, what I had to do, and saw it through, without exemption.
I planned, each charted course, each careful step, along the byway,
And more, much more than this, I did it my way.

Over the Rainbow

from THE WIZARD OF OZ

Music by Harold Arlen
Lyric by E.Y. "Yip" Harburg

G   Em   Bm7   G7   C   D°7   Cm

E7   A7   D7   Am7   G6   Am6

Strum Pattern: 3
Pick Pattern: 3

Verse
Moderately

1. Some - where o - ver the rain - bow, way up high,
2. Some - where o - ver the rain - bow, skies are blue,
3. *See additional lyrics*

there's a land that I heard of once in a lull - a - by.
and the dreams that you dare to dream real - ly do come

To Coda

true.

Bridge

Some - day I'll wish up - on a star and wake up where the clouds are far be -

hind me. _____ Where trou - bles melt like lem - on drops, a -

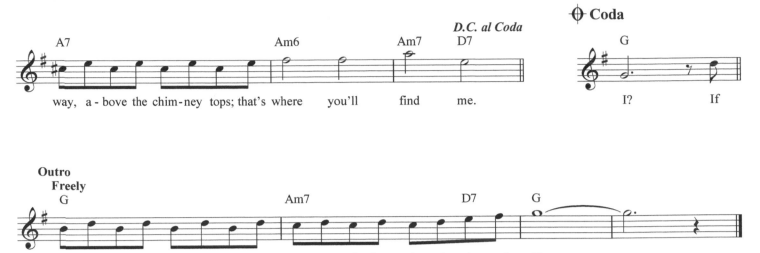

way, a- bove the chim-ney tops; that's where you'll find me.

I?   If

Outro
Freely

hap- py lit - tle blue-birds fly be - yond the rain-bow, why, oh, why can't I? _____

Additional Lyrics

3. Somewhere over the rainbow,
   Bluebirds fly.
   Birds fly over the rainbow,
   Why, then, oh, why can't I?

Send in the Clowns

from the Musical A LITTLE NIGHT MUSIC
Words and Music by Stephen Sondheim

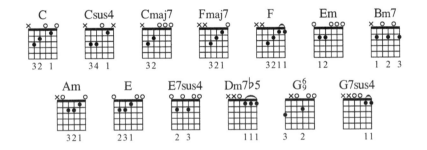

Strum Pattern: 8
Pick Pattern: 8
Slow, in 4

Verse

1. Is- n't it rich? Are we a pair? Me here at
   bliss? Don't you ap - prove? One who keeps

last on the ground, you in mid - air... Send in the clowns.
tear- ing a - round, one who can't move... Where are the

Piano Man

Words and Music by Billy Joel

Strum Pattern: 8, 9
Pick Pattern: 8, 9

Verse
Moderately

1. It's   nine   o'-clock on ___ a   Sat-ur-day,   the   reg-u-lar
2., 3., 4. *See additional lyrics*

crowd shuf-fles ___ in. ___   There's an   old   man ___   sit-ting   next   to   me ___

___   mak-in'   love   to   his   ton-ic   and   gin.

He   says,   "Son,   can   you   play   me   a   mem-o-ry? ___   I'm

not   real-ly   sure   how   it   goes, ___   but   it's   sad   and ___   it's   sweet   and   I

Additional Lyrics

2. Now John at the bar is a friend of mine, he gets me my drinks for free.
And he's quick with a joke or to light up your smoke, but there's someplace that he'd rather be.
He says, "Bill, I believe this is killing me," as a smile ran away from his face.
"Well, I'm sure that I could be a movie star if I could get out of this place."

3. Now Paul is a real estate novelist, who never had time for a wife.
And he's talking with Davy who's still in the Navy and probably will be for life.
And the waitress is practicing politics, as the businessmen slowly get stoned.
Yes, they're sharing a drink they call loneliness, but it's better than drinkin' alone.

4. It's a pretty good crowd for a Saturday, and the manager gives me a smile.
'Cause he knows that it's me they've been comin' to see to forget about life for a while.
And the piano sounds like a carnival and the microphone smells like a beer.
And they sit at the bar and put bread in my jar and say, "Man, what are you doin' here?"

Satin Doll

Words by Johnny Mercer, Billy Strayhorn and Duke Ellington
Music by Duke Ellington

Strum Pattern: 4
Pick Pattern: 1

Verse

1. Cig-a-rette hold-er which wigs me, o-ver her shoul-der, she digs me.
2. *See additional lyrics*

Out cat-tin' that sat-in doll. _____

Bridge

She's no-bod-y's fool, so I'm play-ing it cool as can be. _____

I'll give it a whirl, but I ain't for no girl _____ catch-ing

me. _____

Additional Lyrics

2. Baby, shall we go out skippin'?
Careful, amigo, you're flippin'.
Speaks Latin, that satin doll.

3. Telephone numbers, well, you know,
Doin' my rhumbas with uno,
And that 'n' my satin doll.

Skylark

Words by Johnny Mercer
Music by Hoagy Carmichael

Somewhere

from WEST SIDE STORY

Lyrics by Stephen Sondheim
Music by Leonard Bernstein

Strum Pattern: 3, 4
Pick Pattern: 2, 4

Additional Lyrics

2. There's a time for us,
Someday a time for us.
Time together with time to spare,
Time to learn, time to care.

Some Day My Prince Will Come

Words by Larry Morey
Music by Frank Churchill

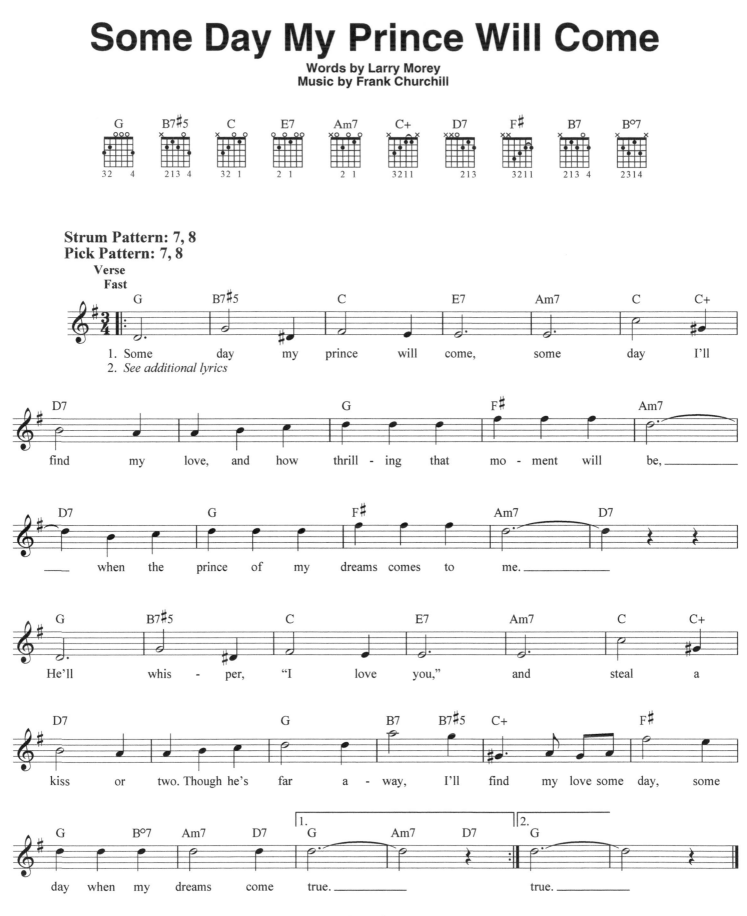

Strum Pattern: 7, 8
Pick Pattern: 7, 8

1. Some day my prince will come, some day I'll
2. *See additional lyrics*

find my love, and how thrill-ing that mo-ment will be, _____

_____ when the prince of my dreams comes to me. _____

He'll whis-per, "I love you," and steal a

kiss or two. Though he's far a-way, I'll find my love some day, some

day when my dreams come true. _____ true. _____

Additional Lyrics

2. Some day I'll find my love, someone to call my own,
And I'll know her the moment we meet,
For my heart will start skipping a beat.
Some day we'll say and do things we've been longing to.
Though she's far away, I'll find my love someday,
Some day when my dreams come true.

Someone to Watch Over Me

from OH, KAY!

Music and Lyrics by George Gershwin and Ira Gershwin

Strum Pattern: 3
Pick Pattern: 3

Verse
Moderately

1. There's a some-bod-y I'm long-ing to see. I hope that he
2., 3. *See additional lyrics*

turns out to be some-one who'll watch o-ver me. _____

me. _____ Al-though he may not be the man some girls think of as

hand-some, to my heart he car-ries the key. _____

me. _____

Additional Lyrics

2. I'm a little lamb who's lost in the wood.
   I know I could always be good
   To someone who'll watch over me.

3. Won't you tell him, please, to put on some speed,
   Follow my lead, oh, how I need
   Someone to watch over me.

Stardust

Words by Mitchell Parish
Music by Hoagy Carmichael

Additional Lyrics

2. You wandered down the lane and far away,
   Leaving me a song that will not die.
   Love is now the stardust of yesterday,
   The music of the years gone by.

Stormy Weather
(Keeps Rainin' All the Time)

from COTTON CLUB PARADE OF 1933

Words by Ted Koehler
Music by Harold Arlen

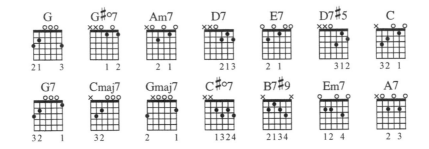

Strum Pattern: 4
Pick Pattern: 4

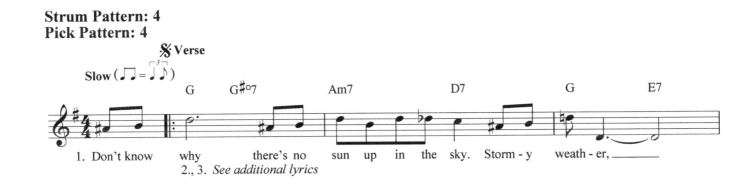

1. Don't know why there's no sun up in the sky. Storm-y weath-er,
2., 3. *See additional lyrics*

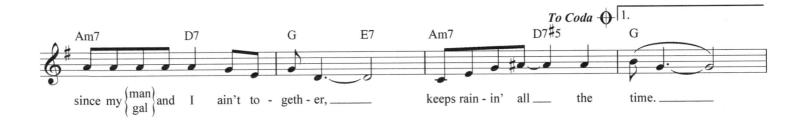

since my {man / gal} and I ain't to-geth-er, keeps rain-in' all the time.

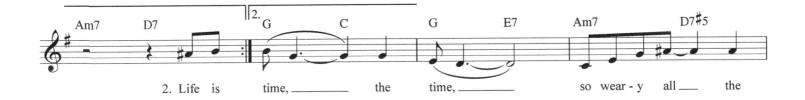

2. Life is time, the time, so wear-y all the

time. When {he / she} went a-way the blues walked in and met me.

D.S. al Coda

If {he}{she} stays a-way old rock-in' chair will get me. All I do is pray the Lord a-

bove will let me walk in the sun once more. 3. Can't go

⊕ Coda

time, _____ keeps rain-in' all ___ the time. _____

Additional Lyrics

2. Life is bare, gloom and mis'ry ev'rywhere.
   Stormy weather, just can't get my poor self together.
   I'm weary all the time, the time,
   So weary all the time.

3. Can't go on, ev'rything I had is gone.
   Sormy weather, since my {man}{gal} and I ain't together,
   Keeps rainin' all the time,
   Keeps rainin' all the time.

Summertime
from PORGY AND BESS®
Music and Lyrics by George Gershwin, DuBose and Dorothy Heyward and Ira Gershwin

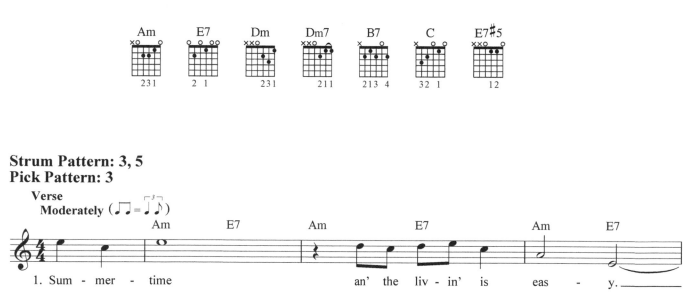

Strum Pattern: 3, 5
Pick Pattern: 3

Verse
Moderately

1. Sum-mer-time   an' the liv-in' is eas- y. ____

Unchained Melody

from the Motion Picture UNCHAINED

Lyric by Hy Zaret
Music by Alex North

Strum Pattern: 4
Pick Pattern: 2

Chorus
Slow

Oh, my love, my dar - ling, I've hun - gered for your touch a

long, lone - ly time. Time goes by so slow - ly and

time can do so much. Are you still mine? I need your love,

To Coda ⊕

I need your love. God speed you love to

Bridge

me! Lone - ly riv - ers flow to the sea, to the sea,

See additional lyrics

2nd time, D.C. al Coda

⊕ Coda

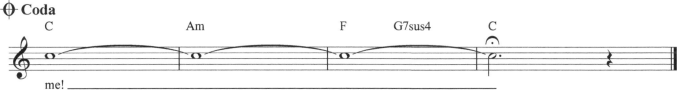

Additional Lyrics

Bridge   Lonely mountains gaze
At the stars, at the stars,
Waiting for the dawn of the day.
All alone, I gaze
At the stars, at the stars,
Dreaming of my love far away.

The Very Thought of You

Words and Music by Ray Noble

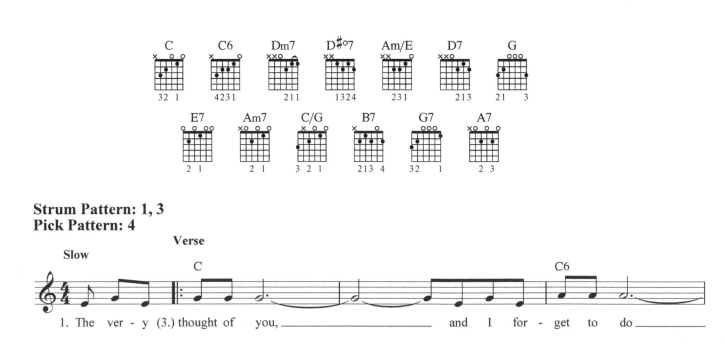

Strum Pattern: 1, 3
Pick Pattern: 4

Verse

Slow

1. The ver - y (3.) thought of you, ____ and I for - get to do ____

Tears in Heaven

Words and Music by Eric Clapton and Will Jennings

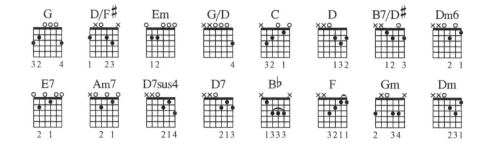

Strum Pattern: 1
Pick Pattern: 2

Verse
Moderately slow

1. Would you know my name _____ if I saw you in heav-
2. Would you hold my hand _____ if I saw you in heav-
3. Would you know my name _____ if I saw you in heav-

en? Would it be the same _____ if I saw you in heav-
en? Would you help me stand _____ if I saw you in heav-
en? Would you be the same _____ if I saw you in heav-

Chorus

en? (1., 3.) I must be strong _____ and car - ry on _____
en? (2.) I'll find my way _____ through night and day _____
en?

_____ 'cause I know _____ I don't be - long _____ here in heav - en.
_____ 'cause I know _____ I just can't stay _____ here in heav - en.

They Can't Take That Away from Me

from SHALL WE DANCE

Music and Lyrics by George Gershwin and Ira Gershwin

Top of the World

Words and Music by John Bettis and Richard Carpenter

Additional Lyrics

3. Something in the wind has learned my name,
   And it's tellin' me that things are not the same.
   In the leaves on the trees got the touch of the breeze,
   There's a pleasin' sense of happiness for me.

4. There is only one wish on my mind,
   When this day is through I hope that I will find
   That tomorrow will be just the same for you and me.
   All I need will be mine if you are here.

Unforgettable

Words and Music by Irving Gordon

Strum Pattern: 4, 6
Pick Pattern: 4, 6

Verse
Moderately

1., 2. Un - for - get - ta - ble, __ that's what you are, __ un - for - get - ta - ble, __

__ tho' near or far. __ Like a song of love that clings __ to me,

how the thought of you does things __ to me. Nev - er be - fore __ has some - one been more __

__ un - for - get - ta - ble, __ in ev - 'ry way. __

And for - ev - er - more, __ that's how you'll stay. __ That's why, dar - ling,

it's in - cred - i - ble that some - one so un - for - get - ta - ble thinks that I am

un - for - get - ta - ble, too.   too. __

We've Only Just Begun

Words and Music by Roger Nichols and Paul Williams

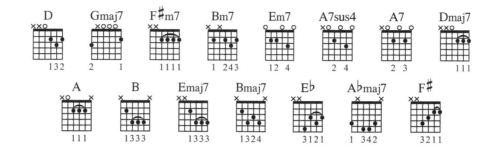

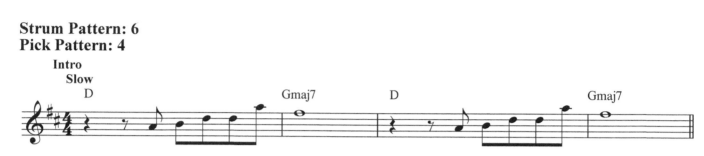

Strum Pattern: 6
Pick Pattern: 4

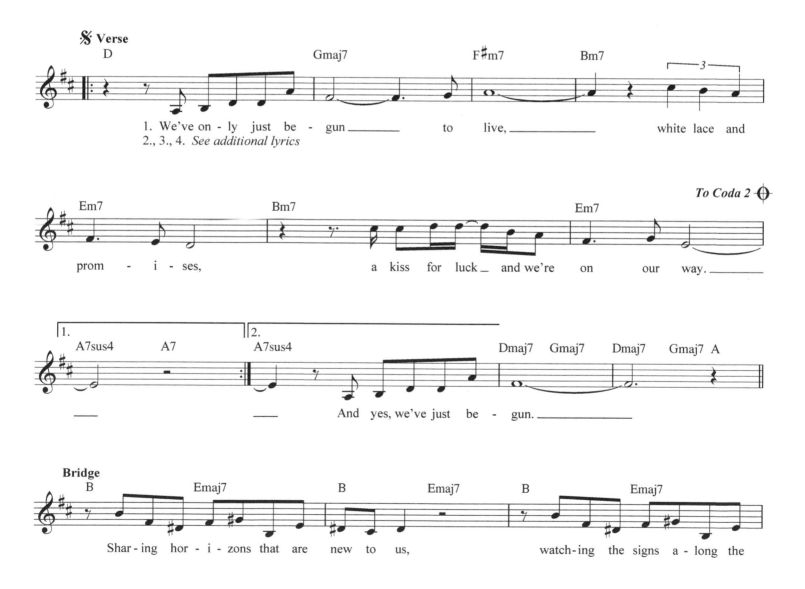

way.   Talk-ing it o - ver, just the two of us,   work-ing to-geth-er day to

To Coda 1 ⊕   *D.S. al Coda 1*   ⊕ **Coda 1**   *D.S. al Coda 2*
                       (take 2nd ending)

day,   to - geth - er. _____   geth - er, _____   to - geth - er. _____

⊕ **Coda 2**

_____   And yes, we've just be - gun. _____

Additional Lyrics

2. Before the rising sun we fly,
   So many roads to choose,
   We start out walking and learn to run.
   And yes, we've just begun.

3., 4. And when the evening comes we smile,
   So much of life ahead,
   We'll find a place where there's room to grow.
   And yes, we've just begun.

What a Wonderful World

Words and Music by George David Weiss and Bob Thiele

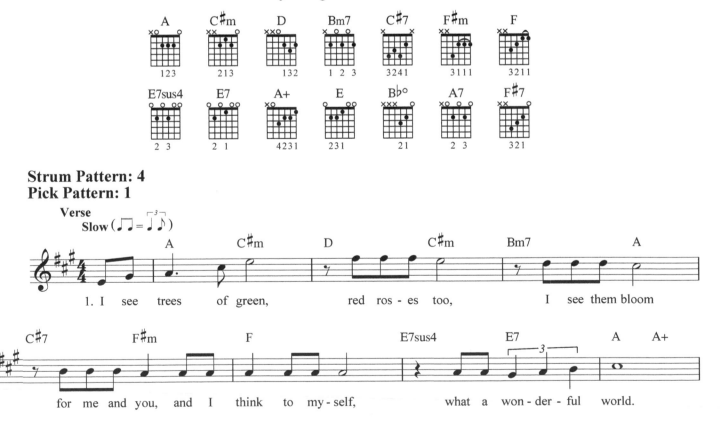

Strum Pattern: 4
Pick Pattern: 1

1. I see trees of green,   red ros - es too,   I see them bloom

for me and you, and I think to my - self,   what a won - der - ful world.

Additional Lyrics

3. I hear babies cry, I watch them grow;
   They'll learn much more than I'll ever know.
   And I think to myself, what a wonderful world.
   Yes, I think to myself, what a wonderful world.

What Is This Thing Called Love?

from WAKE UP AND DREAM

Words and Music by Cole Porter

took my heart _____ and threw it a - way.   3. That's why I

Verse

ask the Lord _____ in heav - en a - bove,   what

is this thing _____ called love? _____

When I Fall in Love

from ONE MINUTE TO ZERO

Words by Edward Heyman
Music by Victor Young

Strum Pattern: 1, 3
Pick Pattern: 2, 3

Verse
Moderately

1. When I fall in love, it will be for - ev - er,

or I'll nev - er fall in love. _____   In a

When You Wish Upon a Star

Words by Ned Washington
Music by Leigh Harline

Yesterday

Words and Music by John Lennon and Paul McCartney

Strum Pattern: 1, 3
Pick Pattern: 2, 4

Additional Lyrics

2. Suddenly, I'm not half the man I used to be.
   There's a shadow hanging over me.
   Oh, yesterday came suddenly.

You Are So Beautiful

Words and Music by Billy Preston and Bruce Fisher

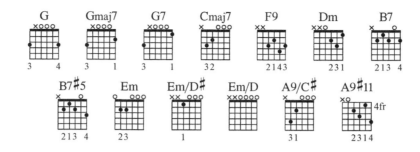

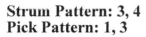

Strum Pattern: 3, 4
Pick Pattern: 1, 3

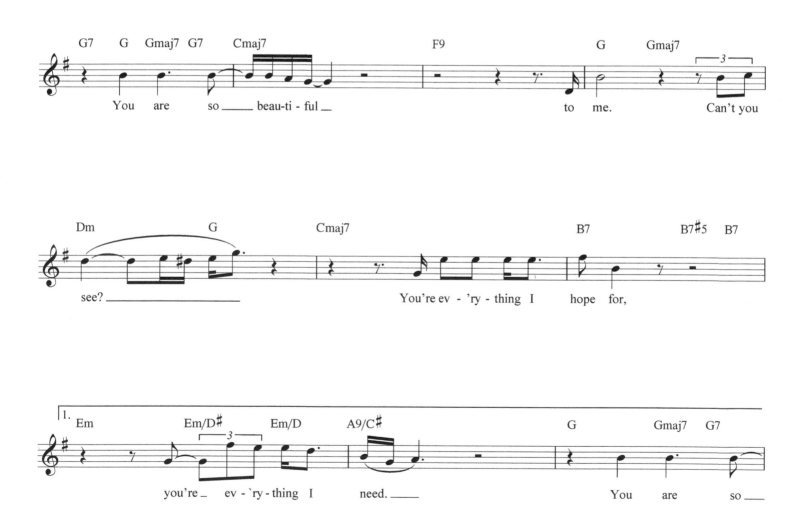

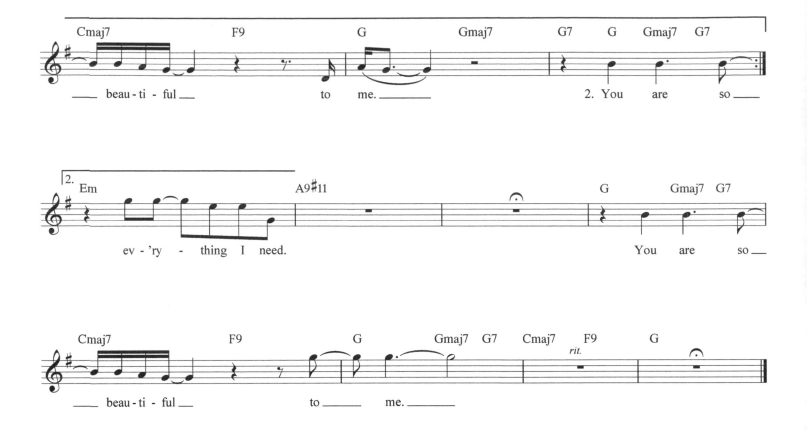

beau-ti-ful ___ to me. ___ 2. You are so ___

ev-'ry-thing I need. You are so ___

beau-ti-ful ___ to ___ me. ___

You Are the Sunshine of My Life

Words and Music by Stevie Wonder

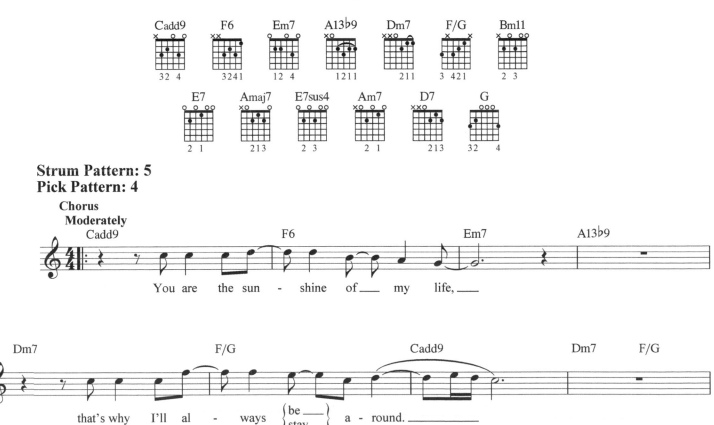

Strum Pattern: 5
Pick Pattern: 4

Chorus
Moderately

You are the sun - shine of ___ my life, ___

that's why I'll al - ways { be ___ / stay ___ } a - round. ___

Additional Lyrics

2. You must have known that I was lonely
   Because you came to my rescue.
   And I know that this must be heaven;
   How could so much love be inside of you?

You've Got a Friend in Me

from TOY STORY

Music and Lyrics by Randy Newman

Additional Lyrics

2. You've got a friend in me.
   You've got a friend in me.
   You got troubles, then I got 'em too.
   There isn't anything I wouldn't do for you.
   If we stick together we can see it through.
   'Cause you've got a friend in me.
   Yeah, you've got a friend in me.

You Raise Me Up

Words and Music by Brendan Graham and Rolf Lovland

C   Csus4   F   Gsus4   G   Fadd9   Am

Strum Pattern: 1
Pick Pattern: 5

Verse
Moderately slow

When I am down ___ and, oh, my soul so wea-ry, when trou-bles come and my heart ___ bur-dened be, then I am still ___ and wait here in the si-lence un-til you come and sit a while ___ with me. You raise me

Chorus

up so I can stand on moun-tains. You raise me up to walk on storm-y seas. I am strong ___ when I am on ___ your shoul-ders. You raise me

up to more than I ___ can be. You raise me up be.